The Many Faces of Domestic Violence

A Woman's Guide from Trauma to Triumph

Sheri Durricks, MHSC, LCADC

THE MANY FACES OF DOMESTIC VIOLENCE: A WOMAN'S GUIDE FROM TRAUMA TO TRIUMPH

Interior Design: TamikaInk.com

Photography: Ed Ward, III- Legacy Studio

ISBN-13: 9781517741952

This book was printed in the United States of America.

Testimonials

"Sheri's book is very well done. The minute I started reading it, I knew exactly what I was looking for. This book is clear and concise and offers much more information than I expected. As a counselor, I feel that we must be the best we can be for the sake of our clients and for our well-being. I must tell you that reading Sheri book has helped me to understand more about domestic violence. This book is written for everyone because everyone is a potential victim. It is a must read."- **Jonas Akpasse, MSW**

"It is likely that you or someone you know has been plagued by debilitating effects of domestic violence. You should feel safe in your relationships. The Many Faces of Domestic Violence is inspiring, thought provoking and empowering to all those who have been demeaned by the debilitating effects of this social and emotional injustice. This is a must read for you and those you love"- **Rev. Ronald Davis, MHS**

"*The Many Faces of Domestic Violence* is a must-read book for every person out there. Sheri does an excellent job through her personal experiences helping us understand the reality of domestic violence and how it affects each one of us. If you or someone you know may be a victim of domestic violence, this book will teach you how to recognize the signs, what to do about it, and give you the hope and plan you need to create a better, safer future."

-Sherica A. Matthews,
Author of, "Engineering Faith."

"*The Many Faces of Domestic Violence,* is an exciting read from teaching women to soul search and then arming them with tools to win during their pain. I highly recommend this book to women everywhere who are struggling with loving themselves enough to live."

Tracy Crawford

Honoring the Legacy of Those who moved from Earth to Glory

In Honor of the late Bishop O. T Jones Junior Holy Temple Church of God in Christ, thank you for my beginnings. I was in search of something to satisfy the longing of my soul, and your ministry of prayer help me to navigate through this journey called life.

In honor of the late Dr. Marlene D, Tally a General in the Kingdom. Thank you for how you allowed the Lord to use you throughout the years. Some of your most powerful messages that blessed me were, it's all in how you see it, I have the Victory and the Victory has me and trusting an all-knowing God to an unknown future. These messages will forever impact the lives of many and echo all around the world.

In honor of a General in the Kingdom, Richard D. Henton who was been called from labor to reward. Thank you for the years that you have been a blessing to my spiritual father Apostle Kenneth Porter and his congregation. I have a CD that I purchased of you praying and I will forever be blessed… Rest well Grandfather

In honor of Pastor Judy Gibbs, I know you're in heaven smiling upon us. I miss your laughter and jokes. You were truly a remarkable person and you will always be missed.

In honor of Aunt Margaret, Hello Walls…. who could ever forget this saying... In other words, listen and pay attention. You will forever be missed…

Dedication

Dear Heavenly Father,

Thank you for choosing me to be a vessel for your glory. Thank you that despite all my imperfection, you continued to bet on me. Your promises are forever settled in heaven and your word has not returned void, but it has accomplished the thing you sent it to do.

Several years ago, I found myself out of your will in a relationship that was not orchestrated by you, but you did not turn me over to the plan of the enemy. I told you that I would do whatever you asked of me and here we are. Now I know what it means when you say that you would exceed my expectations.

I recognized that the safest place to be is in the will of God. Thank you for making me to lie down in green pastures, leading me besides the still waters and restoring my soul. I now understand what you mean when you say that the thoughts that you have of me is good and not of evil to bring me to a bright and beautiful future. Yes, I see my future and it looks better than my past. Thank you so much for all your love and kindness towards me.

I return to you the gift that you have given me and ask that you bless me to write this book, so that the lives of many women will be saved. Thank you for choosing me.

I love you with everything in me. You are the air I breathe and every breath I take is because of you, without you I can do nothing.

Acknowledgements

To my mother and best friend, Lottie Durricks, who is the greatest example of a strong woman. You have taught me how to go after the things I desire in life because of your notable example. I'm the woman I am today. You are a single mother of five, yet your children experienced the best education, clothes, housing etc. Mom you are the GREATEST!

To my Pastor and spiritual father, Apostle Kenneth Porter, who is one of the greatest examples of what it means to be consistent in God. You have taught me so much and many of the things that I'm doing today is because of how you have inspired me throughout the years. In addition, you are the father I never had. Thank you for all the years you Pastored and fathered me.

To my Sisters Joyce, Phyllis, Brenda, and Patricia, thanks for all your encouragement to those who supported me throughout the years. Evangelist Annie Jones, Evangelist Juanita Jefferson, Pastor April Barfield, Evangelist, Camille Forest Darcel Jones, Renee Mahoney, Evangelist Tracy Crawford, and Judith Robinson Thank you for all the years of your support and love.

Most of all I like to give major KUDOS to my business and life coach, Shalena D.I.V.A. Broaster. You have been one of the most inspiring women that I have connected with. To everything there is a time and season to every purpose under the heavens. I must say God has connected us for such a time as this and I appreciate you allowing God to use you to help so many women unlock their dreams. Continue to walk in your purpose. Love you much!

To the former President of Young Women's Christian Counsel local and west District of Common Wealth of Pennsylvania COGIC Juanita Jefferson. As a young woman you mentored and taught me and countless other young women how to be servants in ministry and how to execute the word of God. Thank you for your love and support throughout the years. I'm anxious to read your book that is coming soon

To all the young women who have crossed my path throughout the years and allowed me to mentor, teach and empower you. Thank you so much…Every one of you make life worth living. Thank you for trusting me with your darkest secrets and those things dear to your heart. Although you have learned many things from me, I have learned so much about myself while working with you. My purpose became clear because of our connection. I'm forever grateful...

To women everywhere of every race, culture and ethnicity this book is for you. It's not too late. God has a purpose for you and now is your time to experience the life that you always dreamed of free from mental, physical, verbal and emotional abuse. Remember you are the captain of your own ship. There are many women that have fallen into troubled waters and did not have faith, knowledge, or ability to swim to shore, but if you are reading this book, it is a sure sign that you're ready to swim for shore. Every decision you make from this day on will determine your future. I see your future and it looks better than your past. Ladies, I say to you Talitha Cumi, which means Woman Arise!

Table of Contents

Chapter 1: Understanding Domestic Violence............ 1
Chapter 2: The Perfect Picture....................................... 39
Chapter 3: The White Pickett Fence............................. 71
Chapter 4: The Face of Shame 98
Chapter 5: Abuse of Power 111
Chapter 6: The Holy Hush 116
Chapter 7: The Silent Epidemic 125
Chapter 8: Starting Over 140
Conclusion 154
References 156
Credits... 158
About the Author.. 159

Dear Reader,

It is with great joy and enthusiasm that I have this opportunity to share my first self-help book, *The Many Faces of Domestic Violence.* Thank you so much for purchasing my book. As you read many of the stories in this book, you will discover many things about yourself. Many of the stories will assist you with self-discovery, identification of your own personal and internal struggles, and awareness. This book shares the stories of different women...both their struggles and triumphs. In addition, you will gain insight, knowledge, and resources that will assist you with your personal journey.

Below is a list of a few things I desire for you:

- First, is that you finally take action
- Conquer your fears
- Embrace your freedom
- Stand in your God given Authority

This is what Faces is all about, finally taking Action to Conquer, Embrace and Stand. The Many Faces of Domestic Violence was written with you in mind. Although I share various stories, this is my personal story about how I overcame mental and emotional abuse and my personal journey to loving and accepting myself. Over the years I have learned how to do the internal work, which meant I had to look into the mirror of truth and deal with my personal truths. This was necessary so that I could become a better me *to* me. During this process, I discovered that I was seeking for external love, acceptance and validation only to discover what I was looking for was on the inside of me.

Yes, I realize that I hold the key to my own personal happiness. You see, many times when we are seeking for a mate, significant other, boyfriend, boo or whatever we label them, most of the time we are looking for somebody to make us happy. Happiness comes from within. I did not know this in the beginning. I had to learn that I hold the key to happiness and the person I connect to will only compliment me. He will compliment the Sheri that has learned to fall in love with herself. I now enjoy my own company, I know how to go out by myself and not feel insecure and isolated. Don't get me wrong it's nothing like hanging out with the special someone. Every woman would enjoy that, but it is great when you can be healed within and realize your own value and worth.

Ladies you come with a price tag. You are not a simple commodity for men to use abuse or take advantage. I remember my pastor, Kenneth Porter, preaching one Sunday morning and he gave an illustration about the finest gems.

You know when you're looking for a nice piece of jewelry? You go into the jewelry store and you look in the glass case admiring the beauty of all the fine jewelry, but the most expensive and finest jewelry is found in a vault in the back of the store.

Now it comes down to how much you're willing to pay for the piece of jewelry you want to purchase. The jewelry displayed in the case in the front of the store is expensive and you may get a discount, but the jewelry in the vault you must pay the full price. I remember my Pastor saying to me, "Sheri, stay in the vault because somebody is going to come by and pay the full price for you."

What was my pastor saying? You won't be devalued or discounted because you're the full package and someone is willing to honor you for the pure diamond, or gem that you are. Ladies you are a rare valuable gem. A gem is fines polished stone or pearl fine enough for use. It is like unto to a prize as such a stone because of its beauty and worth. Think about the process that a gem goes through before it is presented in all its beauty. You have been through the process called life and no matter what you have been through you survived and you have a story to tell.

Perhaps you're just simply ready to escape the abuse because you know the Creator has more in store for you. I'm here to assist you on this journey. If you have come out of abuse and don't know what to expect now, I will give you practical steps to teach you how to move forward and heal. You maybe presently in an abusive situation and want to come out but don't know how. I will give you a safety plan and my workbook will teach you how to develop your own safety plan.

Lastly, this book is written with the intention for you to become transparent and for you to use your voice. You see abuse can break your spirit, silence your voice, and isolate you from those who love you the most.

Ok Ladies, it's time to get connected, let go of your past, forgive, discover your voice, tell your story and unlock your dreams, gifts and talents!

Chapter One

Understanding Domestic Violence

Domestic violence and abuse can happen to anyone and is often overlooked, dismissed, excused or denied. It is often associated with visible bruises, black eyes, or a physical appearance of some type of mark, cut, or scar. However, it is much more than that. Domestic violence destroys family, diminishes an individual's self-worth, wounds one's spirit, isolates, dominates, causes economic deprivation, elevated levels of stress, which can exacerbate any chronic health issues that may already exist, depression, and sadly it is one of the leading causes of death.

Despite these few facts, even when the relationship has ended, the psychological and emotional consequences of violence can be as serious as the physical effects.

You see, when a woman is abused it's not just restricted to her. The abuse perpetuates a cycle of violence. More than likely the children have witnessed the abuse which means they are at a higher risk of becoming abusive as adults. Due to the abuse, children are also at a higher risk for physical and mental health problems; this includes drug and alcohol.

Children model what they see, and in later years of their life they repeat the cycle. 40% of girls age 14-17 report knowing someone their age that has been hit or beaten by a boyfriend. One in five female high school students have reported being physically or sexually abused by a dating partner, so understand that domestic violence will affect your children.

Dating Violence

Domestic violence has many faces; dating abuse is a major problem among our youth both male and female. Ladies you may not be an actual victim of abuse, but your daughter or son may be in trouble. Abuse found among youth includes physical, emotional, verbal and sexual. Sometimes it is hard to detect because the abuse does not reveal the physical signs of a black eye or bruises. Anytime a child is experiencing stalking, harassment, verbal abuse, and frightened of the person they are dating, it is time to seek help.

Teens that experience abuse or dating violence are at risk for a variety of negative outcomes. They are four to six times more likely to become pregnant than their peers. One study reported low self-esteem and emotional wellbeing, more suicidal thoughts and attempts, and more likely to have eating disorders.

Parents, friends and other caring adults should know the signs that a teen is experiencing dating violence:

- Suspicious bruises or other injuries,
- Failing grades, loss of interest in activities or hobbies that they once enjoyed
- Excusing their dating partner's behavior
- Need to respond immediately to calls or texts from their partner and or fearful around their partner
- Involvement of a partner who is much older than the teen is at risk for experiencing forced sex
- Other signs that suggest that your teen may be at risk of perpetuating dating violence:

- Insulting their partner
- Controlling how boy/girlfriend act or dresses
- Consistently texting or sending instant messages to monitor behavior of their partner
- Losing temper or unable to control anger
- Threatening to hurt themselves or partner in case of a breakup

If you observed violent behavior or suspect that someone you know is involved in dating violence, act immediately. Below are some helpful resources:

The National Dating Helpline

1-866-331-8453

TTY 1-866-331-8453 for the hearing impaired. Live chat is available, and texting assistance is accessible by texting love is to 77054.

Parents your child may be resistant because they want to hold onto the relationship, they hold onto excuses to justify their behavior and stay in the relationship. Sometimes they feel the behavior is their fault or that they can change the individual. Abusers often mask what they do behind a joke or say they were provoked.

"My intuition tells me something is wrong, but I seem to bypass the red flags"-Sheri

When you're dating or in a relationship with someone it is not easy to detect the early stages of individuals exhibiting violent or abusive behaviours. Domestic violence intensifies overtime. The abuser often appears to be the gentleman, very charming, almost perfect at first, however, as the relationship proceeds, the abuser become more aggressive, and controlling. The abuser also demonstrates some behaviours that may be easily disregarded or minimized. For example, they may start with isolating you from those you love, name-calling, threats, possessiveness, or distrust such as accusing you of cheating, questioning what you wear, or making you feel inadequate because of what you wear.

He may start off with saying things like, "Who you getting dressed for? Oh, you are looking for another man to holler at you."

Women who have children and have gained weight may hear, "Look at you, your fat, ugly, no one will ever want you." Or, "Who is ever going to want you with all those kids?"

Perhaps you may be the individual who have not completed school, and have a hard time making ends meet. Then you find yourself depending on this man to take care of you and your children and he uses finances as a way of controlling you. This is all part of domestic violence and characterized by the game called intimidation, control, and power.

Intimidation, Control, and Power.

Ladies, intimidation is used to create feelings of fear, awe and inadequacy in you. I say it's a game because the abuser is very strategic in what he does. Think about a game of Chess. Chess is a game of strategy and tactics which has three stages. In the opening, the player brings out their forces in preparation for combat. Think about when you initially date someone. The middle game starts with the player's maneuverings for position and carrying out attacks and counter attacks. The final stage is when fewer pawns and pieces are left on the board, it is safer for kings to come out and join the final battle. As the game proceeds, each play will capture some of the opponent's men; the capturing pieces are immediately recaptured. If the piece the player gives up is generally equal to the piece he gets in return, this is what is called exchanging. If you unintentionally place a piece where it can be captured without getting a piece equal in return, it is called *en prise,* which is a French term literally meaning *in take*. Sometimes a player may place en prise to trick an opponent.

Now the objective of intimidation is to restrain you from action and coerce or force you into submission. Intimidation wants to overpower you with a sense of inferiority and fear. Once you have retreated into submission, either knowingly or unknowingly, you are a servant of the intimidator. You are no longer free to be who God created you to be for his purpose, but you are enslaved to the desires of the intimidator.

The abuser may apologize profusely for their actions or try to convince the victim that they do these things out of love or care. However, keep in mind that violence and control always intensify over time with an abuser, despite apologies. What may start out as something that was first believed to be harmless such as wanting to spend all his time only with you because they love you so much, escalates into extreme control and abuse like threatening to kill or hurt you or others if you speak to family or friends. The abuser now controls you so that he can get you to do whatever he wants you to do.

Remember I told you that abuse is not always easily detected. Think about when you initially date someone and the two of you begin by trying to figure each other out. You look for certain things to determine the character of the person you are dealing with. Sometimes we miss little subtle things because we may be intrigued by how good he looks, how much money he spends, the car he drives, the way he walks, talks and the sweet nothings he whispers in our ear.

The Initial stage of Dating: Manoeuvring for Position

In the beginning he is extremely attentive, you get the consistent calls and texts, and suddenly you become the object of his affection. He begins to tell you, "I know it's a little too soon, but I'm really feeling you babe and we should probably step it up and move in together. I want every waking moment to be all about you. I want to build a future with you."

He smothers you with gifts and sends flowers to the job, and you feel like such a queen. He is jealous and protective, which interprets possessive. You like this because you think it's cute and flattering but, he is positioning himself into your heart, so that he can gain your trust. You feel a little uneasy about how fast it's moving, but don't want to mess things up...after all the other guys never took this type of interest.

Ladies, you must be cautious and can distinguish when someone is really a good catch as opposed to having meaningless intentions. This does not mean if you meet a guy and he does and says all the right things that he is abusive. It does mean that if you're vulnerable, just getting out of a relationship, always attracting the wrong man who devalues you, unhealthy self-esteem issues, and your validation comes from how a man sees you, and then you need to be cautious. You may miss the red flags because you haven't gotten rid of your own personal baggage. Understand that when you don't work on yourself emotionally, spiritually and mentally, your spiritual antennas may be dull, and you miss the flags you're supposed to pay attention to.

Ask me how I know? Because I missed many red flags because of my own personal issues which I will discuss in Chapter Two. There are many red flags to look for. For example, listen when he begins to discuss his former relationships or marriage. Does he blame others for the failure of the relationship? Does he degrade his ex's character or call them names like, "My ex is a bitch, stupid, or a liar, and I'm so glad I met you. Finally, I met somebody who understands me."

You fall for this as he continues to shower you with gifts, but it's different this time. You notice that he is buying you personal items like clothing and jewels that is not what you normally wear. He tries to stop you from seeing your friends by professing his love for you saying things like, "Baby you know how much I love you. I just want to spend time with you."

He says, "its love," but in all actuality he is slowly isolating you.

Seeds of Self-Destruction – Harvest of Self Doubt

I call this next section, "Seeds of self-Destruction," which is planted by the abuser, so that you begin to doubt yourself. You must be careful what you disclose about yourself in a relationship. Many times, we tell too much too fast or we disclose things that should be our own personal secret. When you disclose information about your past relationships, you give the enemy (your abuser) tools to work with. You may say things like, "In my last relationship my ex was not as attentive as you, and he didn't buy me gifts like you."

You share everything that your ex did not do, and you disclose it to a potential abuser, rest assure he is going to do the opposite to gain status with you. Once he gains status with you, he subtly begins to sow seeds of self-doubt. He says things to you that are demeaning when the both of you are alone such as your hair does not look right, your clothes are too revealing, or you look like a slut, but when he is around your friends he uses the same demeaning terms and masks it as a joke.

He targets your appearance so that you can begin to feel less attractive. Remember I told you earlier that it's all about strategy. His tactics are subtle so that when you confront him he gets offended because he's trying to make you believe that he is joking. My Pastor always taught me that many things that are said in jokes are what people really mean. There's an old saying that out of the abundance of the heart the mouth speaks. In other words, you will discover what's in an individual heart by what comes out of their mouth.

He begins to insult your friends and tries to plant seeds of discord in your heart towards them. He is moody and unpredictable. This is what I call the *Dr. Jekyll and Mr. Hyde syndrome*. One minute he's happy and the next minute angry. This is where the blame games come. He blames you for his mood so that you can start adapting your behaviour to please him. This is called subtle control. He accuses you of cheating on him or flirting with other men. He ignores you by starving you from getting his affection and then when you please him he rewards you by giving it back. All of this makes you a prisoner of self-doubt, which produces additional insecurities. Now you are unable to make concise decisions on your own. You begin to seek him in making the decisions no matter how great or small.

Escalation of Abuse

He has already conquered you subtly, now he takes it a step further. He begins to hit, smack and punch you and minimizes it by saying, "I didn't mean it. I love you so much. I just lost it because I can't imagine losing you."

The previous things I mentioned have already broken your spirit and now you're subject to the physical abuse. He apologizes to you and tells you he will never do it again and you forgive him, but he doesn't stop there. Next, he gets a hold of the finances and you are totally dependent upon him. He blames you for everything that happens wrong which plants seeds of self-doubt, you believe him. He becomes more physically and verbally abusive and repeats the same old apologies because he has convinced you that he will change. You begin to make excuses for his behaviour and start to blame yourself. "If I had not done this or that he would have not done this or that. If I do better in this area he won't be upset."

It's a never-ending cycle with you jumping through hoops to make him happy. When you talk of leaving him, he immediately threatens to hurt you, the children and himself. Once the abuser gets you to doubt who you are and your ability to stand on your own you become a captive of his tactics. You are now afraid, isolated, and afraid to say anything fearing you might say something that will set him off. Women who were once strong, vibrant, independent, and happy are now timid and fearful.

Now that you have read this section, what are some of the red flags you notice in your relationship?

____

____

____

____

____

Now that you have identified the red flags, what is your plan of action?

____

____

____

____

____

____

The most damaging aspect of abuse is the trauma to our heart and souls from being betrayed by the people we love and trust

- Robert Burney

Financial Abuse

I would like to shed some light on financial abuse. Financial abuse is one the most common tactics used by the abuser to gain power and control. Like other forms of abuse, it starts off very subtle. For instance, information regarding financial accounts may be concealed and you will no longer have privileges to use credit cards or there will be extreme limitations on how or what you are able to spend. In conjunction with the other types of abuse mentioned, financial abuse is used to entrap you. You may be going through this now or when you decide to leave the relationship. As I stated some financial abuse is subtle. The abuser will stop at nothing to keep you as a victim from working or having access to funds.

Perhaps your reading this book, and you have decided to get out, but you're afraid because you don't have a job, lack education, skills, transportation, the children are depending on you, or you feel that you lack resources to assist you. At the end of this book, I will connect with resources to help you. Although finances are a needed source for you to provide for yourself and children, please don't let that hinder you from your choice. Your abuser will be sure to use this tactic because it is one of the most powerful methods of keeping you trapped and diminishing your ability to stay safe after leaving the relationship. I have assisted many young women who have children. Yes, it was one of the most frightening decisions they ever had to make, but many succeeded at doing it. You see you must do it, so that your children will not perpetuate this cycle and so that you can live to be everything God created you to be. Here are some warning signs to look for.

- Prohibiting Employment. A subtle way of doing this is, “Honey I know you’re under a lot of pressure with the kids and all, so stay home and I’ll take care of the household.” It can also be more abrupt where he totally forbids you to work.
- Sabotaging work or employment by stalking or harassing you at work. He will constantly call the job, threaten other staff members if he can’t talk to you. Therefore, causing you to be terminated from your job.
- You once had access to the accounts now he has restricted your use. He makes comments like, honey your spending too much money, or I lost my debit card, so I

needed to close the accounts and re-open another.

- Withhold money and giving you allowance
- Running up large debt on joint accounts
- Stealing your identity, property or inheritance. This is done to deplete you and ultimately destroy your credit worthiness.
- Refusing to pay or evading child support,
- Manipulating the divorce process by delaying the process or hiding assets
- Forcing you to give up your pay checks
- Stealing money from you or your family
- Withholding physical resources like food, clothes, necessary medication or shelter.

- Forces you to cash in, sell or sign over financial assets (e.g. bonds stock or property)
- Force you to agree to the power of attorney so he can sign legal document
- Force you to work in family business for little pay

If you feel that this financial abuse applies to you, here are some additional tips. If your partner has access to your credit card statement, social security number or other pertinent information that identifies you. It will make it easier for him/her to open accounts in your name or continue to access your accounts. Also, they may use your children's information to open accounts. If this is you, then you must consider being proactive and keep your information safe.

- Call your banking institution and credit card company and ask for your account numbers, PIN numbers, passwords and other access code to be changed.

- Use passwords that would be hard to figure out.
- If you're using your personal phone, computer, tablet or iPad, make sure it is safe, so that the abuser does not attempt to install spyware.
- Lastly, you may also want to consider enrolling in a reputable credit protection program through your credit card company or banking institution.

The scars I can't see are the hardest to heal- Astrid Alonda

Internal scars are the hardest to heal because you can't address what you cannot see. You act out with certain behaviors, but do not fully understand it's a result of what you saw, experienced or are currently going through. After spending many years in an abusive relationship, your concept about self becomes distorted. You start to believe what you were "taught" about you. Remember when someone abuses you, their tactics are intentional. They want you to feel less than nothing, shirk, without confidence, weak, timid and afraid, so that you fear them and become forever submitted to their **control**.

He is your master and you are his slave. Whatever orders he/she gives you; it would be in your best interest to obey. The lack of obedience to an abuser infuriates him because he must have control. You may have been a victim of childhood abuse. You may have watched your mother get beat or verbally abused and wonder why you keep ending up with men that abuse you. You grew up watching or experiencing it, and then the behavior becomes normalized.

Everyone has a belief system which is attached to events that happen in our life. "Our belief system creates a perception. It sends an electrical signal to our hypothalamus in our brain which produces the chemical that match our perceptions. The chemical, called peptides are than distributed throughout our body. This creates the emotion that matches our perception about the event. There is a peptide for anger, love sadness, love, happiness and every emotion we experience. When we encounter an episode at the hand of an abuser that matches an already existing childhood wound, our brain triggers feelings of powerlessness, victimization, worthlessness, and other fearful perception. We literally regress to the emotional age of our original wounds. In addition, we create mental defenses around our inner wounds if they are not directly healed."- Melanie Tonia Evans

I remember mentoring young lady years ago and her dad would have pounds of marijuana in the house. This young lady went to her friend's house and said she would wonder why her friend's parents did not have bags of marijuana sitting around. She thought this was normal. I had a friend who lived three doors from my former house. She was in a domestic violence situation; her live-in boyfriend would beat the crap out of her and she equated the beating as love.

One day I witnessed him beating her and I certainly thought she would leave. Instead of leaving she told me, "He beats me because he loves me."

One of my former clients had a sister who died. She had become sexually involved with her sister's boyfriend after the death of her sister. He infected her with a STD (Herpes or Syphilis) and brutally beat her. She went to court, got a restraining order, which only lasted for a brief period. She continued in the vicious abusive cycle.

Do you see how such acts can become normal? I worked with and mentored many women like this. It's important to deal with our scars from the past, but it's hard to address what you cannot see. All we know is that we exhibit strange behaviors that we cannot explain, or we tolerate behaviors from others that should be unacceptable.

Perhaps you're reading this, and you say, "None of this applies to me; I had a perfectly good childhood, make good money and have a good career."

Don't be fooled. You are not exempt. In fact, some abusive men search for you because you're strong, intelligent and independent. You are a challenge to them and they take pleasure in breaking you down. Later in the book you will read stories about other women who all share similar experiences. Domestic violence does not discriminate and has one common denominator for all women who are and have been victims; there is a perpetrator who chooses to abuse his victim whether it is physically, emotionally, verbally, or mentally it all constitutes abuse and victims comes from all walks of life.

While the physical abuse is apparent, the invisible scars can last a lifetime if not addressed. Emotional and verbal abuses are examples of invisible scars. Although it does not manifest the physical appearance of black eyes or bruises, it can be far more damaging and can have a serious impact on your self-esteem, confidence, health and overall well-being. Verbal and emotional abuse is also a form of ***Power and Control.*** If you are involved with someone who is constantly yelling, insulting you or calling you derogatory names, you are being emotionally and verbally controlled, which can impact you mentally.

Why? Because you begin to look at yourself through a different lens and find it hard to express or even believe in yourself. Emotional abuse causes you to question if you're capable of doing anything correctly while verbal abuse plays a constant tape in your head reminding you about things you would like to forget. Words have power and if you believe the words that your abuser speaks, you bring life to that which is evil. These evil words can and will be a destruction to your production in life and very soul.

I'm a therapist and I have worked with teens, adolescence and women; many are of low socio-economic status and live in deplorable neighborhoods. Due to their living conditions, I naturally thought that domestic violence had restrictions. Don't be fooled it's not restricted to one culture, race ethnicity, or economic status. Many have or will be affected: it's your doctors, lawyers, nurses, corporate, and school teachers, they come from all walks of life and have great professions.

I remember looking at the news about a year ago and a husband and his wife were both doctors and shared the same practice. Patients were scheduled for appointments but could not get in because of all the cops on the outside. After many hours, it was discovered that there was a murder/suicide. Many of the patients said that they were shocked because this was the nicest couple and there were no signs of trouble. As time went on, it was revealed through the media that this wife was a victim of domestic violence.

Many times, questions are asked, "Why don't victims come forth?" or better yet, "Why do they stay? What makes them silent about their dilemma?"

Women have many reasons why they won't report when they are physically, emotionally, and mentally abused. Some are embarrassed, fearful, and economically dependent upon the abuser. You see, in some cases you have women who are involved with men of power and authority. These men are well-known and hold high status in the community such as your judges, lawyers, doctors and even pastors. Sometimes this makes these women more reluctant to speak out for the fear that people will not believe them. Unfortunately, many have died never having the courage to break the silence. The number of women murdered everyday by a current or former male partner in the United States is 38,028.

There is a metaphor about boiling the frog. The premise is that if a frog is placed in boiling water, it will jump out, but if it is placed in cold water that is slowly heated, it will not perceive the danger and will be cooked to death. This is the ideal description of a woman in an abusive relationship.

"When one Survivor speaks out, we all Break the Silence"- Anonymous

Don't be afraid to talk about what's happening with you, you are not alone. Speaking the truth about domestic violence is healing for all. Take courage today and own your voice. There are many stigmas that are attached to those of you experiencing this type of violence. Shame and guilt is a feeling that everyone has experienced at one time or another. We feel guilt when we feel responsible for an action that we regret. Shame takes place when we feel disappointed about something inside of us our basic nature. Both emotions have intense implication for how you perceive yourself.

Now is your opportunity to not only speak out for you, but someone else will get the courage to use their voice and tell their story? During fall 2014, headlines about domestic violence and sexual assault dominated the news provoking conversation and awareness about this critical issue. Shortly after, NFL players were the focus because of the abuse some common with these men. Many former and current players came forth to shed light on this hidden crime. Several had personal experience with the issues,

including Troy Vincent, NFL Executive Vice President of Football Operations whose mother is a survivor of domestic violence and Pittsburgh Steelers
Quarterback, William Gay, whose mother was killed by an abusive partner.

You're not alone. Take Courage, speak out, and tell your Story. Meet me in Chapter 2, as I share my story.

Confession

Speak this out of your mouth, let it germinate in your heart, and watch it work in your life…

Father, I thank you for giving me the spirit of wisdom and revelation in the knowledge of you. I thank you for opening the eyes of my understanding, that I might know what is the hope and plan that you have for me, and the exceeding riches of your eternal glory. The exceeding greatness of your power resides in me because I believe. I believe that you have already filled me with the knowledge of your will in all wisdom and spiritual understanding that I may walk worthy of you unto all pleasing, and fruitful in every good work increasing in the knowledge of you. I agree with your purpose, plan and will for my life and from this day forth I look forward to my life being forever changed because I trust in you- Colossians 1,9-10

Chapter 2

The Perfect Picture

We all have dreams. I remember as a child playing house with Barbie and Ken. I had a cute little playhouse and I would always imagine me with nice big house, married to a tall handsome man, and children. In a child's mind, this is the perfect picture. As I grew older, I began to have encounters with the opposite sex that I didn't understand. Some of our encounters in life derive from our childhood experiences. Studies have shown individuals who grow up in an environment of abuse or have been sexually abused; they tend to end up in the same situations later in life. Also, girls without fathers tend to suffer from rejection and abandonment issues.

I am the child of a single mother longing for the love of my father. My memories of my dad are not quite vivid, but I remember my dad coming to visit me from time to time. One of my fondest memories was of him playing with me at the playground. I remember me wearing a white dress with colorful flowers eating a cherry water ice. You could not imagine how good it felt to be in the presence of my father. He would pick me up, swing me around and kiss my little tender pudgy cheeks. I would hold on to him for dear life as he swung me in the air. My little legs dangled in the air as they shined from being greased down with Vaseline. What stood out to me the most was how his coarse black beard would rub against the smoothness of my little pudgy cheeks when he kissed me. I felt so loved, secure and confident in his arms. It was the best feeling a little girl could experience.

Dad continued to visit me for a while. During one of his visits, I remember him and my mom arguing. I saw mom pick up a wet red and white dish cloth and hit my dad with it as he blocked the clothes with his arms. Afterwards, I noticed that the visits became less and less. Eventually, there weren't any visits at all. I remember wondering what I had done to make him leave. This separation made me feel lost, lonely, and insecure.

Later, in life, I discovered that dad was a player and had another family. My siblings and I ended up meeting the rest of our extended family after one of my siblings contacted him. He told us where he lived. During this, I learned that dad owned several bars on Popular Street in North Philly. So, I enjoyed popping up at the bar, and hitting him up for money. It became about money for me because I felt dad rejected and abandoned me.

Life continued to move forward. Dad continued to be missing in action. Although dad was not very active in my life, God continued to bless mom to give my siblings and I the best. I attended Catholic school during elementary and some of my high school years; than in the 7th grade I went to a private boarding school in Scotland Pennsylvania, so I grew up with a sheltered but structured and disciplined life.

I graduated in 1983 worked and attended Community College of Philadelphia and briefly attended Pierce University. I did many things that teenagers do and went through the process of life. I share this to highlight the fact that domestic abuse is not restricted to someone who grew up in deplorable conditions or in an environment where abuse is normal. I struggled with depression, and low self-esteem. Because I was so young when dad stopped his visits I encountered many internal struggles.

I felt un-loved and was always afraid of being abandoned or feeling rejected. I didn't really know how to process my feelings, so I thought I'd better be on my best behavior or I would be left alone. I really did not understand this early on, but as I matured I noticed that I always worked hard for love in a relationship with the opposite sex.

We all have what is called preset buttons that are installed at an early age. These buttons are only installed when you begin to ask questions. These questions may begin with something you heard about yourself or an experience you encountered such as, "You're ugly, stupid, fat, skinny, I hate you, or you will never be anything."

What happens later is that you begin to ask yourself "Am I ugly, stupid, fat?"

This simply means that you begin to question you and how others perceive you. I spent many years wondering if I would ever be loved. I hated *me* because I was black, skinny with those short-connected plats in my head. I mean I was shaped like a flat ironing board while all my girlfriends walked around with beautiful voluptuous bodies (LOL). So, in life we carry this childhood baggage which leads us in situations we may not understand.

Sometimes we attract and conform to certain relationships that may not be in our best interest because we have not uninstalled those preset buttons of low self-esteem, abandonment, and rejection. This brings me to the questions many ask. Why do women stay in abusive relationships especially when their life is in danger? I became involved in church when I was in my early twenties. I remember hearing a great message which allowed me to see relationships from a new perspective. During this time in my life, I decided to discontinue dating and learn about me and God's purpose for my life. I spent many years involved with church ministries and decided that I would no longer be sexually involved with anyone until I was married. I was celibate for many years until I met a young man in 2008.

I thought he was a nice, "tall glass of water," that was coming to quench the thirst of a sistah who was waiting for God to bless her with her boo. He was 6"4, black and juicy, bowlegged, very intelligent, educated and very resourceful. He was very charismatic with a great since of humor. In addition, he could cook or burn in the kitchen as we used to say. He could also clean. I remember him coming to my house one night and he made me such a beautiful cuisine. It looked like something you could place in a cookbook.

He had many of the characteristics I was looking for. I thought he was the perfect man and that having him would complete me. We spent much time hanging out and just being good friends without benefits, lol. Remember, I developed an unhealthy view of myself because of my daddy issues and due to my issues with rejection, abandonment, and low self-esteem, I thought, "Wow, he wants somebody like me?"

Things were cool for a while, until I discovered he was a predator, or may I say a womanizer. In Chapter one, I mentioned how I ignored the red flags. Now my first encounter with this man was in Atlanta, Georgia. We were both attending training in pursuit of our career in the field of human services. We had a conversation after the training one day discussing our place of employment only to discover we worked less than 10 minutes from one another. This was the only conversation we had.

As time went on I encountered him again, this time at my place of employment. He was sitting in the office with my supervisor being interviewed for a job. Fast forwarding, I began to train him for the position basically familiarizing him with agency paperwork and procedures. We had to be to work every morning at 10:00 am and for some reason he would appear at my office every morning at 9:45 am giving me all these compliments and I loved it. One day he asked if he could come to my house so that we could go out for dinner. I discovered that he only lived 15 minutes away from me, so I agreed.

He came to the home in Philadelphia and we went out and everything seemed to be fine. We laughed talked and just had fun with one another. After class, he drove me back to my house. He waited for me to get in my house and immediately called me stating that he enjoyed my company. For some reason, I had this gut feeling that he was slick, but I ignored my feelings. I did not trust him, but I did not understand why. I remember going to bed that night praying Lord please don't let me get caught up with this man. He wanted to know too much about me to soon. Although my intuition was telling me something about him, I eventually ignored it and became caught up in the superficial part of him. I never questioned why he wanted to know so much about me so soon, or why he would ask me personal questions about my former relationships, if I had money saved in the bank, he was overly friendly, and took great interest in things I liked.

He knew I loved church and I sang for him one day and he was surprised at that the girl could sing. He started singing and we made good music together. On one occasion, he even went to church with me.

Keep in mind that a predator will take interest in your hobbies or activities so that you can trust them. He was always in my space making me feel so important. He had a way of drawing me to him and throwing me away at his convenience. For instance, we would go out and have a blast for extended periods and then he would disappear and come back later with his charm as if nothing ever happened. He would try to make me feel like it was something I did to make him disappear.

Oh, he was good at playing mental havoc with my mind. He knew that if he disappeared or ignored me for extended periods of time I would surrender to his control when he came back. Mental and emotional abuse is designed to chip away your independence and self-esteem. Don't think for one-minute abusers only choose weak women. Some delight in breaking down strong women. Although I had underlining issues I 'am a strong, black, beautiful, confident and independent woman. I have an excellent job, paid my own bills, drove my own vehicle and lived in my own home, he hated this.

Before I met this man, it was difficult for men to get the time of day with me. I was an inspector of one's character, relationship with God, and prayer life. When I saw red flags, you would be immediately dismissed. I remember him telling me that he admired how I served God but that he was jealous. If that wasn't a red flag! Who would be jealous of your relationship with God? I ignored it because I thought he would change. For instance, if I was going to church he would try to persuade me to stay home, or he would talk about my friends or Pastor so that I would isolate from them.

Abusers are very strategic. They have a way making you feel like you're on top of the world one minute than throwing you to the curb as if you don't matter. They have what I call that Dr. Jekyll and Mr. Hyde personalities. For a man to reduce you, they must first seduce you. I'm not talking about physical seduction. This seduction is persuasive, alluring, as with charm in the way of gifts, and flattery.

Domestic abuse is about **Control** and **Power**. Although I encountered this type of behavior, I continued to be involved with him. On the outside I seemed to have it all together, yet I was in a toxic relationship. I didn't see it at first, but it soon became evident.

We were both pursuing our Degrees at the Community College of Philadelphia. One day we left school together and spent some time together at my house. He eventually went home but later that evening I decided to go to his house. I rang the bell and he would not answer. I thought it was strange because his car was in front of the door. Finally, he answered the door. I asked why it took so long to answer the door. He replied that he was sleep. I noticed that he was blocking the entrance to the door and he did not invite me to come in, so I said, "Babe, I need to use the bathroom."

Just as I was walking into the house he literally threw me to the ground.

My car keys went one way and my body the other. I laid on the ground in shock wondering why.

Now remember he had just left my house a couple hours before this, so there was no reason for this behavior. As I was getting off the ground, I asked him if he had another woman. He proceeded to convince me that there was not another woman in his house and that I was crazy. I was mentally and emotionally drained, tired of his mess and I decided to fight back. I searched for a brick so that I could break his car windows. During my search, the police had arrived, and I decided to press charges and get a restraining order against him.

We were both placed in separate rooms at the police station and I remember feeling so distraught. I wondered why I was accepting this type of behavior. Finally, I was released and went home both angry and broken. The next morning, I got went to church. It was Easter Sunday. Outwardly, I looked good, but on the inside, I was so wounded.

My esteem was at an all-time low. My friends and I talked as usual, but I did not want anyone to know that I was in an abusive relationship. I decided to share it with several of my friends in the church. I remember sitting in the church staring in a daze. The preacher was preaching, the parishioners were getting blessed as they praised the Lord and I was just sitting with a blank stare and no response. You'd think this would have been my turning point. No, I continued in the relationship. Why? I was afraid of being left, and I did not know how to address or heal the childhood struggles of rejection and abandonment that had began to surface.

Children are often disappointed by people, events, and reality, which cannot match their youthful ideals. The wounded little girl inside of me saw this man as my ideal lover. You see, the ideal lover thrives on people's broken dreams, which sometimes become lifelong fantasies. He reflected my fantasy of having the perfect relationship that would make me complete and he was an artist in creating the illusion I required. The way I saw it, I was getting older and I had not been in a relationship for many years. My clock was ticking, and I felt that maybe he would change, and things would get better. This is one major delusion that women think. We become ensnared by our own deceptive thoughts believing, "If I stay he will change or the situation will get better." Maya Angelo said, "When someone shows you who they are, you better believe it."

He was very jealous and competitive. I remember when I enrolled in school for my degree. I had already completed one year. An orientation was approaching, and I was meeting with several colleagues at this orientation. At the time, my place of employment was closing and many of my co-workers were going to be laid off. I told many of them about the program and agreed to meet them at this orientation. He also attended, and I introduced him to the Assistant Director.

The Director instructed him that he needed to take a test as a requirement for enrollment. He took the test, passed and was accepted into this accelerated program. After some time, he told me, "I never wanted to be in this program. I just enrolled because you will never be ahead of me. I will always be on top of you and you will be beneath me."

Remember some of the signs I talked about in chapter one? One of the faces of domestic violence is verbal abuse. He had subtle ways of demeaning and acting as if it were innocent.

The second episode took place on a Friday night; I was home and needed to return some DVD's to the library and was getting into my car when my now ex, walked up to the car and asked, "Where are you going?"

I laughed because I wanted to make him jealous. Suddenly he grabbed me by my collar and snatched me out of the car. It happened so quickly that I did not know how to react. He dragged me to the door of my residence holding my collar. "Open the Door!" He yelled.

I was afraid, so I opened the door and he dragged me to my bedroom. I remember the room being pitch black. He threw me onto the bed, sat on top of me and pinned my hands to the bed.

"I'm sorry, I'm sorry," I said over and over. He never hit me but used excessive force to keep my entire body pinned down. As I was saying, "I'm sorry," I remember him asking, "Do you love me? Tell me you love me!"

Once I assured him that I loved him he loosened his grip, released a deep sigh of relief and laid his body on me. He laid on me as if we had just made love and he was satisfied with the pleasure of just laying on me. For some unknown reason he equated this behavior with love. How sick and distorted.

Another time we were out and parked in my drive way. We got into an argument and he snatched my wig off my head and threw it. I have never felt more humiliated and disrespected.

You may think, "Oh that is nothing," but the invisible scars of mental and emotional abuses are sometimes worse than physical abuse.

His personality transitioned from evil to Mr. nice guy. Then he said to me in a nice calm voice, "I know I exploit women and use them for my own purpose."

When you encounter a man who tells you, *I know I exploit women for my own purpose.* Run!!! Predators know who you are. They smell loneliness, vulnerability, and other unresolved issues. You see, predators possess excellent senses to find their prey; they are very charming and skilled at social manipulation. They are also skilled liars so it's important to always watch their actions.

You know that good old saying, *persistence knocks down your resistance.* This is done so that you can become emotionally dependent on them, and so later they can use what you told them to manipulate and control you. They seem too good to be true and guess what? They are. At the time I was dealing with this individual, he had no problem with using women for money or whatever. He would say and do many things to me, but no matter what he did, he always had a way of charming me right back into the web of madness.

We both had to appear in court because of the restraining order I placed on him for throwing me to the ground. The day of the court hearing we were both holding hands laughing and talking as if nothing happened. I continued in this madness for many years off and on. I would leave it alone for a while then go back, often wondering why I kept allowing myself to be mistreated. I'm in the church serving God, looking good, dressing nice, but never really dealing with my underlining issues or may I say I did not know how to.

What *looks good* to you is not always good *for* you. You are reading this book and you want to come out of your situation, but you don't know how. First, begin by understanding it's possible. I did it and you can too. Lastly, you must let go, forgive, and **Keep It Moving.**

Let the Truth Set You Free

Once I chose to release my past and walk into my future I noticed there was a certain pattern that kept happening in my life. I was attracting the same type of man. As a result, I had trust issues, fearful and mentally tormented. Many times, after leaving a toxic relationship there is resentment, and anger. Despite this, I had to forgive this man. It was not easy, and it was a process. There were times when I would become so angry until I would think of unimaginable things to do to this person.

For a moment I hated men because I had always been hurt by them. I thought "Now every man is going to pay!"

That was the moment I realized that I had become a prisoner to my ugly thoughts and feelings. I hated the way this made me feel and I had to do something about it, so I decided to become better not bitter. God has given me so many wonderful talents. I often notice that I'm good at using and extending my gifts to help others but not myself. There is an old saying, "Physicians heal thyself." Luke 4:23

I have helped and encouraged so many people throughout my life especially women. I discovered that what I released to help others is also the antidote to help myself. When this episode ended, I realized that I really did not love myself. Anything you love you value. What a painful but needed reality check. I allowed myself to be disrespected and treated in a manner that was not productive for my life. I learned my value once I realized how much I *devalued* myself. I began to see me, Beautiful Sheri, through a different lens. I started to affirm to myself only those things that were good. I dealt with the issues of my past, the rejection, fear and abandonment.

I remember the days I felt so inadequate and incomplete. As a little girl, I could not accept being dark and skinny with those little plats [braids]. You know the plats where you could hardly get a barrette on them? Yes, those plats. Because of this I always compared myself to other females that I felt looked better. When you don't love yourself, that energy goes into the atmosphere and you attract others who don't love themselves and are broken.

Deal with your issues. I had to come face to face with mine. I thought for so long, "I'm a good woman, why would he treat me like this when I have so much to offer?"

God began to show me something about me so that I would never repeat this cycle again. God said to me, *"Sheri, before I formed you in the womb I knew you. Fear not I have redeemed you; I have called you by your name, 'Sheri,' elegant, intelligent, unforgettable one of the most intriguing and beautiful woman in the world. I understand the fears and struggles you would encounter while you were in your mother's womb. I made you grow like a plant of the field. You grew up and developed and became the most beautiful of jewels. Your breasts were formed, and your hair grew, you were naked and bare.*

Later I passed by, and when I looked at you and saw that you were old enough for love I spread the corner of my garment over you and covered your nakedness. I gave you my solemn oath and entered a covenant with you, declares the Sovereign LORD, and you became mine. You are no longer a fearful, insecure, little girl. NOW step out in FAITH and BE...BE WHO YOU ARE, FEARFULLY AND WONDERFULLY MADE."

Forgive.

Un-forgiveness will make you sick. I would always get sick with the flu or extremely bad colds. My spirit was broken, and I was emotionally sick. As a result, I gained weight from eating so much. I would call it emotional eating. I had gotten so sick one day I went to the emergency department. When I got there, I told the doctors my symptoms and they admitted me into the hospital. During my stay, I was diagnosed with high blood pressure and type 2 diabetes. Both illnesses are two silent killers. This was a wakeup call for me.

I was previously given a book on prayer that routes demons and one of the passages described an individual with a broken spirit which contributes to a weakened immune system. Ding dong! The light bulb went off and I decided to take my life back. I took my life back by letting go, allowing God to heal me and learning to forgive. I will tell anyone, it was not an overnight process, but time heals all wounds.

Stop Blaming Yourself and Others

As stated above, I had to look me in the mirror of truth and deal with my issues. I could no longer blame anyone for my hurt and pain. People only do what you allow them to do. You teach people how to treat you. Ouch! What a painful revelation.

I forgave myself and the one who hurt me. My freedom was on the other side of me forgiving the one who hurt me. I was sitting in the hospital bed and asked my niece to go to my house and get my laptop. When she came back with the laptop, I immediately signed up for the gym, got a nutritionist, changed my diet and began loving myself again.

Help Someone Else

To make a long story short, I began to reach out and help other women. I formed a women's group at the organization where I was previously employed. Every Thursday we had group therapy for women, there were over 30 women that attended each week and I was able to identify with many of their issues because I experienced it. God never wastes anything. Helping these women was another form of healing for me. In addition, I graduated with my master's Degree from Lincoln University in 2011 and enrolled in Walden University to pursue my PhD. To date, I'm in the 4th year of my PhD program, writing my dissertation and I have been inducted into The National Organization for Human Services Honor Society Tau Upsilon Alpha Walden University Alpha Chi Chapter in recognition of academic and professional excellence in Human Services.

I am a certified domestic violence and sexual assault advocate. I was recently licensed by the state of New Jersey as a Licensed Clinical Addiction Drug and Alcohol Counselor (LCADC) and pursing some of my other dreams. I began to travel and visit places I always dreamed of; one of them was Paris, France. I embrace the joy, peace and love that God has given me as I let go of the pain from my past. If you are currently struggling, affirm this with me.

Declaration

I ________________________ promise to love and cherish myself. I decree and declare that I am fearfully, wonderfully, and marvelously made. I proudly decree that I am a woman handpicked and created for good. I am made in the image of God and in His image created he me female, strong, courageous, fearless, a true reflection of Him. Therefore, I love myself deeply, unconditionally and completely. I am amazing and beautiful. No longer will I be silent. I have a voice, and I will speak. I forgive myself and I forgive you. I'm no longer a prisoner of regret, hurt, guilt shame, rejection or abandonment. Today I have been set free. Free to love, laugh, and smile and be the best me I could ever be.

Chapter Three

The White Pickett Fence

This is for all you ladies trying to hold it down for the sake of the kids and just wanting to keep your family together. You may have grown up in a two-parent home and vowed that you would have the same for your children. Perhaps you never experienced living with both parents but always wanted a two-parent home for your children. Now you're living with your partner experiencing mental, emotional, verbal and financial abuse and you're fearful of leaving. You're afraid because you have been with your boo since high school. He is all you know. You ask yourself, "How I will start over. After all, I don't have a job, he takes care of me and the children, and who would ever want me with my children?'

In this chapter, you will meet Christina. Christina is the face of the young naïve female with two young children living the white picket fence life; However, Christina could never imagine the price she would pay, or the pain she would endure. Be careful what you wish for, you just may get it. Christina is a Caucasian woman who lived with both parents and always dreamed of having the white picket fence life. Her family was very close knit and she was a daddy's girl. Christina describes her dad as her hero, someone she loves and adores. Unfortunately, Christina's father went to work one morning and never returned home. He had a massive heart attack. Because Christina was accustomed to having the love and security of her father, she wanted to find someone that would love her. She was young, in high school, and searching for new love. Follow Christina as she shares her story.

It is hard to sit down and put all of what has happened to me in the past 20 years in words. I believe by sharing my story it will reach people in the world who have experienced the same things that I experienced in my marriage. I got married and pregnant when I was only 21. My father passed away when I was only 17. As time progressed, and I became more mature throughout the years; I realized that I was attempting to fill the emptiness of a male figure.

I was very close to my father as any daughter can be. Our admiration for each other was how I believed life was. It felt safe and the world was softer. I come from a great Italian family and we were so close, but my father always made my life wonderful. A daughter looks up to her father as a large giant figure – sort of like a super hero who can take care of the harmful villains. One day in November all the aspects of my relationship with my father were damaged. It was like every piece of my world broke like glass and I was hit by a huge cannon ball. He went to work one day like any other normal day and I never saw him again.

My father had a massive heart attack behind the wheel of his car. My family was never the same. It was as if we all were broken, and we needed to fill the void in our hearts. I knew I needed the male figure back in my life and I long just to feel the love of that again.

I met my first husband when I was in high school. I knew him from seeing him around school and mutual friends. I was 17 when we first started dating. We were dating for about two years when he had a streak of bad luck. His brother and his best friend died in a bad car accident. He took it hard, and of course I was very devastated too. We were great friends. He was always there for me when I needed a shoulder to lean on.

Two years later, we had another surprise we were going to have a baby. We both were happy and confused at the same time, but we were determined to make it work and be the next happy family with the white picket fence. Within my 13 years of marriage to him there were countless situations of violent episodes. I wanted so much to have that happy old fashion family with the white picket fence.

I'll start from the beginning. The very first time the violence happened. We had moved in together and gotten married by the justice of the peace and got prepared for the arrival of our unborn child. There is a saying that sticks in my head to this day, "You don't know the person until you live with them." How true is this statement?

I started to notice he was staying out late and hanging out with his friends all the time. We were just way too young to become parents and husband and wife. Nevertheless, I was very willing and able to make the mature change to adulthood, but as I look back, he wasn't.

My first violent episode was when I found him in the other bedroom smoking pot. I confronted him, and we started arguing. I could not understand why he was putting up a fight because he was so wrong, He started yelling at me in my face and then he pushed me. I fell back into the wall and I was so devastated and scared. I was fearful not only for me but my unborn daughter. What hurt the most is that he never said he was sorry. This was the beginning of my violent marriage.

Every time he fought me, I would clean up the items he had broken, and I would hide the many bruises on my arms and legs. I believed that if it was all cleaned up and healed it was as if it never happened. My husband started going out and staying out very late at night and sometimes he would not come home at all. I would jump out of my sleep to see if he was on the couch, but my heart would sink because he wasn't there.

He was abusing drugs; marijuana and pills. I knew he was doing pills because he would have seizures when he took them. Now you must remember my daughter and son were in the mix of all of this. My daughter would hear or see me cry, but not say or do anything. She was so young at the time. By the time my daughter turned nine, my husband and I were in a good place and things seemed to be well with us. At least that's what I thought.

I was now 31 and I wanted to have another child before it was too late. Like I said we were doing better. He was becoming more successful at his place of employment and money was not really an issue as it had been in the beginning. So, I got my wish and I became pregnant with my son. After he was born, things took a turn for the worse. He was abusing drugs again, until he passed out at home and stranded my 11-year-old daughter at the hospital when she was visiting me. A few months passed, and I noticed he was staying out all night again.

When I was nine months pregnant with my son, I remember he had fallen asleep on the couch. I was watching TV when his beeper went off. I looked at it and it was a number I did not recognize. I woke him up because it could have been his job calling him. He said it was his friend. He needed him to go over his house because his car was not starting. He left to go to help his, "friend." I was not happy about this, as you could understand; I had just about had it. I thought things were getting better, another child on the way, money is better and now this?

At this point, I am older now and I feel that I have become stronger. It was February and there was ice and snow on the ground, so I grabbed my daughter and her blanket because it's now February with ice and snow on the ground. I didn't care that I was nine months pregnant; I decided that I was not going to put my head in the sand anymore. I drove to his friend's house and the house was dark, so I drove around town, even to his parent's house, but no husband.

Now this is how many excuses I gave this man – I even went to the ER to see if something had happened to him. I was so naïve, but again, no husband. I finally gave in and went home.

I went right to his closet and threw all his clothes in a bag. This was one of the many times his clothes were placed in bags and he would leave and go to his parent's house. It was a pathetic cycle of our fighting and abuse that happened about once a year. I could never understand why his parents would take him in. To me, it made it easier for him to leave me and run home, but they did it and it was an endless cycle that I lived through. I believe this contributed to my insecurities and abandonment issues.

Abandonment is the worst feeling in the world. When someone you love leaves you it hurts like a kick to the stomach. I went back to believing his story and he unpacked his bags because he said he was at his friend's sister's house. The baby was born the next week.

As months went on, I noticed a change in him. He was dressing different and he started to go out again. I could not take how much he would break my daughter's heart when he would go out for the night or go away for work. She would cry so much and beg him not to leave.

One day he went away, and I wanted to surprise him and meet him at the gate at the airport. I went to the gate he told me he would be at and I waited and waited. Finally, the doors opened, and all the passengers came out but no husband. Then the pilots came out. I still looked passed them and saw no husband. I asked the pilots if there was anyone else on plane because I could not believe he was not on this plane. He took the time to give me a gate number and again another disappointment.

I called my mother-in-law at the time and she was also mad at him. He finally came home and told me he was on a later plane. There was another lie. I questioned if I should believe him? I did not believe him, but I stayed quiet. By this time, I was smarter about finding out the truth. I decided to wait and see how things unfolded. A few days later, I went through his car. The first time I did this, I found drugs in his car after he took the last dime out of our checking account to buy them. I could not even buy diapers. The results were another fight, something being broken and him hitting me in the face causing me to bleed. Nevertheless, he sent me flowers with hopes that it would heal my pain, but it never did.

I took a lot of abuse, I kept thinking, I had to keep trying for my children. I wanted to keep the dream alive. I needed to have that dream despite the cost of the mental damage to me and my family. I was too blind to see how it was damaging my children. I just kept trying and trying. I loved him, and I needed to keep us together. Besides, where was I going to go? I had two kids and believe me; I had left him before and gone to my mother's small condo.

This was after another night of abuse and his negative name calling. He would say things like, "You will never be anything in life," or "Who is ever going to want you?"

He was always trying to break me down and assure me that there was no way out but to stay with him. One day I was in his car going through his paperwork. I was looking for bank statements to see if he was spending extra money. I found a note that changed my life forever. Yes, it was a love letter. I read it and was sick to my stomach. It was what I thought had been going on all along.

I confronted him at first, he denied it. Eventually he admitted it, but he convinced me that it was over. He kept reassuring me that she meant nothing, and it was over, and he didn't want to keep it going because he was in too deep. How does anyone cheat when their wife is pregnant? I still ask this question 14 years later. Here I am keeping a clean house, well-dressed children, dinner on the table every night and a great mother. Who does that? I guess some people cannot see the forest for the trees. I continued to try to keep the dream alive. Ladies you can have a huge castle but no one in that castle is happy. Where was I going to go?

My husband got a promotion at work and we were now moving to

Florida. Here's the perfect opportunity to start all over. I thought we could now get away from here and all the negative situations. We moved to Florida and I was happy. I didn't have to work, and I was able to spend more time with my children.

One day, I had dinner on the table when the phone rang; he was calling to tell me he was working late. Yeah, ok, late? I called the office back, but there was no answer. Here we go again. I put the kids in the car and went looking. I drove down the street and saw our car at a strip club. Here goes my heart, my poor heart. It had skipped so many beats it's a wonder I am still alive. I pulled up to the strip club and got out.

I was mad as hell. I opened the door to see him sitting at a gaming machine drinking a beer and of course a stripper on the couch. He almost died when he saw me. He came after me and as I got in the car the stripper comes out and blows him and I a kiss. I don't know to this day if anything happened or she just wanted to have fun with us because she saw us fighting.

I went home and immediately booked a flight home. He begged me to stay and again assured me nothing happened. I stayed because I couldn't even afford the tickets to go back home. I also did not want to call my mother for money. She didn't know anything was wrong in my marriage. I didn't want her to worry about me.

We ended up returning home three months later because I was so homesick. We moved into his parent's house and things started up again; home alone and finding him at bars talking to girls instead of being home. I was very depressed, and I had no job and no money. Where was my life going? I had hit a dead end. There was nothing left. No home, money, job, or hope. Then one day I just could not handle the hopelessness. I found myself in my mother-in-law's living room, alone, with a bottle of sleeping pills in my hand. I wanted it all to end. I was at the end of the road.

As I looked at the pills and tried to figure out how long it would take for me to die, I heard my son calling me from the other room. I snapped out of it as fast as lightening in a storm. In that moment I realized that my storm was about to be over and the sun was going to shine on me. I had hit bottom and there was only one way to go and that was up.

I found a part-time job and began feeling like my independent self again. I had missed her so much. People started to like me, and I noticed how much happier I was. I told my mother that I wanted to stay at her house one day. I told her what was going on and that I could not stay with my husband anymore. It was like a weight lifted off my shoulders. God was with me that sad day and lifted me up.

I sat down with my husband and my mother-in-law and told them I was not happy and didn't want the marriage anymore. He begged me and cried so hard for me to stay. In the past I said, "No. I am done," but I would always stay.

He helped me find a home and even helped me pay for it. I was surprised as much as anyone that our relationship was ending. He wanted to keep a roof over our head. I believe now he did this hoping we would get back together, but it never happened. As a result, he became more violent.

One day he was visiting the kids and he started arguing with me. I don't remember why, but he grabbed me by the throat and started choking me right in front of the children. This happened not once but twice. Another of my many encounters was how I begged the female police officer not to arrest him because she had seen all the bruises on my arms and legs. I was so afraid he was going to beat me or even kill me when he got out. She stated that the department was arresting him, so it was out of my control.

It got bad one day when he came over looking for papers for tax reasons. I told him I would look for them later and asked him to leave. He didn't leave but threatened me and told me to watch my back as he walked out of the door. Passing through the door, he hit me so hard I saw white lights and thought I was going to blackout. I thought he was going to kill me because I was defenseless. I went flying on my daughter's bed and he choked me so hard until I kicked him off me. He ran out of the house and I called the cops and so did he.

He waited outside, and I ended up being arrested because he had a scratch on his face. I just don't understand why. I would have ended up dead if I didn't push him off me. Where is the line drawn? When is it considered self-defense? I could have been another victim of murder. I also believe he put that scratch on his face to this day. So here I am shackled to the wall of a police station and booked. The charges were dropped.

He continued to make my life a living hell. He took my car and my children away from me after lying and to the police stating I tried to run him over. I could not see my children for five very long days. I had to get a lawyer to get them back.

He could not **control** me anymore. Remember Domestic Violence is about

Control and **Power**. He tried so hard with his bullying and the verbal abuse. He kept trying to break me down throughout our entire marriage. As time went on, his words bounced off me. I felt like superman getting hit with bullets. It is so true that the mental abuse can be just as powerful as the physical abuse. Bruises heal, mental abuse does not. This is what is called the invisible scars. I thought this would last a life-time. It still affects me to this day. I don't know but maybe this marriage did affect me and that is why I am still single? Nevertheless, I am working on this by going to therapy. Any abuse is traumatic, so I would highly recommended therapy. I also read up on self-help books and the readings of how you have awakenings throughout your life.

I know what it is like to have an awakening – it happened that sad day my son saved my life by calling my name. I try everyday to understand why he did what he did and why I stayed all those years. I know it was the drugs and his issues and demons he was fighting, but what hurts the most is that he does not even remember most of the abuse. I am the one carrying it through my life like old luggage. Some days I pull it out of my closet and open it and other days I try to forget it's there. Many of you reading my story may wonder why I stayed.

Why I Stayed

I stayed in my marriage because I wanted to keep the dream. You can have a huge castle but no one in that castle is happy. I did not know where I was going to go. I was brought up in a very close family and I wanted that to be the same with my family. I wanted my children to have a father in their lives. At the time, I didn't have all the reasons in my mind;

which clouded my judgment and I didn't realize the damage it was doing to my family.

Life Lesson

I have learned a lot from everything that has happened to me. I learned to be strong, determined, and most of all to believe in myself. I look back at the darkest day of my life when I was going to commit suicide and I realize that I am breathing because God sent his angels to save me from doing such a horrible thing.

I basically woke up and I never ever had that feeling of being trapped anymore. It was an amazing awakening. I had this euphoria of strength and endurance within myself. I was determined to get my life together by myself. I found that person that I knew before I was married. I found the will power to make it on my own. I knew the journey would be a rough ride, but that didn't phase me. I found myself strong again. God was helping me to become the person He intended for me to be. I knew what I needed to do to get my life back. I had to start over again and I eventually took my career from a part-time job to management to district manager. I rented a three-bedroom house with a pool. It took me 2 years to get there but with the determination I finally did it.

Believe

My advice to anyone that has experienced any of these trials and tribulations; you need to know one word.... BELIEVE!! Believe in yourself, believe you can walk on your own, and believe you can have your life back. Believe in God because He answers prayers. There will be days when you don't know how you are going to get through it, but you must believe in God and His path for you. Find support from family, friends and others who have been abused and you will see you are not alone.

REMEMBER THIS!

When you get into a tight place and everything goes against you to the point that it seems you cannot hang on a minute longer. Never give up, that is just the place and time that the tide will turn.

Declaration

I have a Declaration and I would like for you to look in the mirror and say it daily:

I ______________________________

choose to believe in myself. It is my responsibility to guard the safety of myself and my children. I no longer fear leaving because God has not given me the spirit of fear, but of **POWER**, **LOVE** and a **SOUND MIND.** I am not a failure or less of a person because I made a mistake. I forgive myself. Success and failure are part of what makes me who I am. As a result, I'm developing my own character and identity. I am **POWERFUL, CREATIVE** and **ASSERTIVE** when necessary. I will no longer be timid. I am **BOLD and COURAGEOUS,** I have all the **CONFIDENCE** I need to believe that I can do anything. My mind is transformed by the Power of God and I can do **ALL THINGS** through Him that strengthens me. I am **CONFIDENT** and **OPTIMISTIC** about my future. I **BELIEVE** that God is transforming my brokenness and lovingly carrying me from darkness to light.

Chapter 4

The Face of Shame

You see, I'm that cute little girl with the pretty face that everyone adored. Mom had me when she was 33 years old. I've been told that when I was born, mom just held me with so much admiration. She was so proud to hold this little baby for the first time. I grew up in a close-knit home with both of my parents. We are the type of family that sits down at the table to eat dinner every night and are very affectionate to one another.

During high school, I was very ambitious and always excelled in anything I set my mind to do. My greatest passion was running track and I was very good at it. In addition, I was an honor student and the first black homecoming queen in my school. I did not have many friends because girls did not like me, so I was selective with the few friends I had. My best friend and I did everything together. After high school, we separated from one another and enrolled into different colleges. It all happened so fast, I was growing up and had no time to slow down. I graduated with my diploma and before I knew it I was packed up and shipped off to college.

I was young, sheltered and opened to this new world filled with new people and new experiences. I went through my freshmen year with ease, produced good grades, made great friends and I still possessed my innocence. I set boundaries for myself and would not go outside of certain parameters. As time passed, I decided to move off campus and get a place of my own.

Once I moved into my own place, everything changed. I hung out with my roommate; other friends and partied like a rock star, drank and created what I thought would be a lifetime of memories. Suddenly things began to shift, school got expensive, my god mother died, I just had surgery and I was dealing with medical and personal issues. I just could not cope.

As a result, I became depressed and my thoughts were not clear. So, one night I decided to party not to have fun, but to escape from the hurt and the pain that was plaguing my mind and stealing my peace. To forget, I started the night with a Long Island followed by six shots of Grey Goose, two shots of Hennery complimented by one glass of Wine. I thought I was fine, yet I could hardly stand. You know how it is when you're young? I felt strong, and invincible, "I GOT THIS," was my mindset.

I remember trying to get up thinking, "If I can only make it to the bathroom." I began to murmur under my breath and noticed that I was being watched by my roommate's boyfriend. I had previously had an encounter with him trying to flirt with me and I felt very uncomfortable. I rejected his flirty notions on several occasions.

Although I was drinking I could still sense that he was waiting to make a move. I remember seeing him across the room with the red cup in his hand drinking – just watching me. I needed to use the restroom, so as I proceeded to walk toward the restroom I noticed he was following me. When I entered the bathroom, I turned to shut the door when he forced himself in and slammed the door behind him.

He began to have his way with me. I remember struggling trying to defend myself for a while, but the alcohol seemed to be weakening my muscles. I was so afraid. He was much bigger and stronger. All I remember is helplessly hitting the floor. The last thing I remember saying is, "NO, STOP, THAT HURTS, HELP!"

I had no recollection of penetration, or anything. When I woke up the next day, I was sick from the alcohol and I had bruises. After this episode, I went to the gynecologist. Remember I had no recollection of what happened only bruises. So, when I went to the gynecologist, she checked me and gave me a strange look before asking me if I had multiple partners. I answered, "No."

My vagina had been severely ripped causing my uterus to drop and I had to get treated once every two weeks with injections and treatment for Chlamydia. I tried so hard to remember what happened that night, so I began to pray and investigate. I want you to know prayer works. Remember I told you earlier in the story that I didn't have many girlfriends because of the jealousy issues I always encountered with females? My roommate and several other female friends pledged into a sorority, her boyfriend also pledged. I don't know what that pledge was about, but something was wrong.

I asked my friends if they knew what happened to me and showed them the bruises. The party had taken place at our apartment and they were present. No one seemed to hear anything or know what happened. So, my roommate asked her boyfriend what happened, and he lied and said I seduced and came on to him. As time went on, I continued to see my gynecologist, I prayed and researched.

After investigating the situation, I discovered that Saline was put into my drink. Therefore, I could not remember before and after, but not during the sexual assault. My roommate and our other friends immediately betrayed me. They would bully me with threats stating that I better not report the incident to the police. They would also wear dark black clothing on the campus at night using tactics of intimidation to scare me.

You see now this changed my life forever. I feel like my innocence was completely taken from me. Meet me, my name is Lyric, but I'm now the face of shame. Now I'm secretly damaged and walking around with a tattered image of myself and the way men view me. Shame makes you feel lonely, isolated, sad and most of all worthless. Often our feelings are simple reactions to specific events that we perceive as pleasant or unpleasant. Once these events are over, the related feelings fade away. It's not hard to notice that our emotions are fleeting and impermanent. However,

Shame does not work this way. Shame constantly reminds us of our defects and if you're not careful, you will become a continual victim of shame-based thinking.

This is what I did. I continued to blame and have a distorted perception of myself and how men viewed me. After this traumatic event, I suffered from anxiety attacks. I believe that the attacks were triggered because of my unconscious mind remembering the assault, but my conscious mind forgetting because the pain was so intense. As a result, I did not trust anyone, but myself and my gynecologist because she took care of me. I was afraid to hug or be affectionate with anyone and I isolated myself from everyone.

This is the face of shame – it speaks loudly and causes you to focus on your failures daily. Every day you constantly tell yourself that you are defective. My thoughts were constantly plagued with scattered thoughts of judgment and images of impending failure. Therefore, it's important to seek help if you have ever been a victim of sexual assault.

Journey to Healing

Initially I suffered in silence. I did not tell anyone about my experience for over a year. During that time, I also grew angry and I did not trust anyone around me. There was a time when I did not want to be physically close to anyone. Even hugging someone bothered me. I started having anxiety attacks frequently, night by night. It wasn't until I spoke out and started to tell my story that I was able to begin to heal from the trauma.

Don't misunderstand me. Trauma can really affect your life. Therefore, it's important to seek therapeutic intervention; good healthy friends and family that you know are supportive, empathic, understanding, and non-judgmental. I had to learn to trust again and I eventually came out of seclusion. This was accomplished through journaling and prayer.

Life Lesson

To the young girls in college I would like you to know that everyone is not who they seem to be. Not everyone is there to be your friend and make memories with you. Some people don't have your best interest at heart and yes, there are bad people in this world. Always keep your eyes open and be aware of your surroundings. Always hold high standards for yourself. Although you're grown living on your own, it's good to set boundaries and to have accountability partners. If you ever feel unsafe or uncomfortable in a certain setting, leave right away and never be afraid to call campus police or dial 911 if you need help. Also tell a friend or family member don't be silent. Learn to use your voice, speak out and tell your story.

Achievements

Since my experience I have been able to speak to young girls all over concerning domestic violence and sexual abuse. I now have two major titles, Miss Black America New Jersey 2014-2015 and Miss Black US Ambassador New Jersey 2016. I am also in the process of writing a book on my own story and experiences. I have become a stronger and confident person throughout this entire experience.

Now that you learned a little about me. I would like to leave this prayer with you. Repeat this aloud:

Prayer of Faith

Dear Heavenly Father,

Before I was known to man you formed me in my mother's womb and declared that I am good. You created me in your image breathed your breath of life in me, so that I could discover all the beautiful gifts, talents and purpose you have for my life. I am not a mistake you have created me with a purpose. I surrender myself fully to your will, purpose and plan for my life and I let go of every negative thought, hurt and memory from my past.

Heal and cleanse me from every demeaning and self-destructive thought that would make me a prisoner to pain, physical and emotional bondages. Wash away any fragment of shame that would impede my progress. I embrace your peace, comfort, and love that you freely give to me. Surround me with wise friends and counselors who will assist me with this healing process.

Father I pray that you would remove the feelings of powerlessness, fears and threats that hinder me from speaking out and give me the grace, courage and boldness to speak out. Thank you for restoring every area of my life and over throwing the plans that the devil has against me.

I know the thoughts you have of me are good and not evil to bring me to a brighter future. Amen

Chapter Five

Abuse of Power

As children we grow up looking to authority figures to guide us through this journey called, "Life." From a very young age we are taught to obey, respect and listen to those who are in authority such as our parents, teachers, policemen, etc. Children learn how to think independently and how to respond emotionally in situations. As a result, children cannot help but trust in others especially parents and those in role of authority to care for them and look out for their best interests.

Because children need to be able to trust, they are vulnerable to manipulation, exploitation, and abuse by adults, teenagers and other children. Surprisingly so, adults are also subject to the same. The abuse of power is prevalent in our society. Through media coverage you hear about the abuse of power from teachers, priests, pastor's policemen, and coaches. The abuse of power consists of one using their position in an abusive way. For example, gaining information that is not privy to the public, and manipulating an individual with the ability to punish them if they are not compliant.

One of the most common, but silent abuses of power is in the church. Many individuals go to church seeking solace, answers, understanding, and peace of mind, support and hope; however, many women have encountered just the opposite. Reverend Pamela C. White says that pastors are held in high esteem and should practice a good code of ethics, which includes certain boundaries with members. The clergy role carries a significant deal of power in and of itself and is one of the most insidious aspects of that power in the role of, "Man of God."

Ministers have ultimate spirituality and authority, particularly in the eyes of trusting members. Members often look to ministers for spiritual guidance and support. Furthermore, as a man he carries the power. Society look upon men and socializes them to hold over women, often in the guise of being a protector. He is often physically stronger and more imposing. Because of this type of power, ministers should not become involved with their parishioners.

I say this if the intent is to manipulate, exploit, or use his power in an unethical manner. Pastors have an opportunity to emphasize a power *with* rather than power *over* model in the church. However, sexual relationships with female members reinforce traditional male power dynamic and breed a closed destructive parish model. The pastor has an opportunity to validate the gifts and talents of his parishioners, but when he focuses on a woman's sexuality whether he denigrates her other abilities, those talents are discounted. Frequently, the very talents that attracted him to her in the first place became discounted and devalued by him once the sexual relationship began.

Lastly, when a pastor violates member boundaries, he takes away the church's appropriate, powerful and sustaining spiritual guidance and, support. Because of the threats to her reputation, she is robbed of an important arena for her creativity and contributions. Many victimized women report that not only have they lost their parish community, but trust can be so violated that they cannot go to any church at all.

Chapter Six

The Holy Hush

Domestic violence is becoming more prevalent in the churches everywhere. Too often women are afraid to speak about it because their husbands or significant others are in key positions and may be very powerful within their community. For fear that no one will believe them. They keep silent and live in the shadows of fear, shame and isolation. I'm Talaya. I had a daughter at a very young age and I experienced some challenging times as a young girl.

My mother was struggling with an addiction and as a result, my siblings and I ended up in foster care. This was a very hard time for me because I was very close with my mother. I felt a sense of loneliness and abandonment. You know at an early age you bond with your parents – especially mom. When that bond is broken, what's next? Although I had some challenges in my life, I learned how to pray and seek God. My mother had her struggles, but she is a praying woman. Prayer got me through many of the tough times I encountered.

Because of praying I decided to get involved in church and seek after the joy and peace I so desperately needed. Eventually I joined a church and the pastor of this church took notice of me. Now I was currently involved in a relationship with someone. The pastor told me that I needed to break up with this gentleman because *he* was my husband. Now, this pastor was not my type at all, but every time I went to church he reminded me that he was my husband.

At the time I was young and naïve. So, I initially ignored the pastor and continued my relationship with my boyfriend. One day during the service he sent an usher to get me out of the service and beckoned me to his office. When I enter his office he said, "You insist on being disobedient."

I just looked at him. He then said, "God is going to show you in dream that I'm your husband."

At first, I did not believe him, but that night I had a dream, and, in this dream, he was presented as my husband. You must be careful and learn to guard your ear and eye gate. If someone can get into your ear, they have access to your spirit. People can speak subliminal messages to you and you think about it until it happens. The mind is busy, you can actually dream what 's in your subconscious. That's what I did.

At the time I was very young and zealous in the Lord and all I wanted to do is please God. Understand predators prey on your weakness. He must have studied me and knew that I would be someone that he could manipulate. He continued to be persistent and eventually I gave in and began a relationship with him.

Lord, I had no idea what I was about to encounter. He presented himself as if he loved me and I was his prized possession. He took care of me in every way possible. You see young girls are impressionable. We like to be wined and dined, so he uses things to keep me happy. He would lavish me with the finest of things. I had a lovely home, car, clothes, and jewelry. Nothing was too much for him to give me. In addition, I became the first lady of the church.

It seemed quite intriguing to be the first lady of his church. So, I moved in with him and the drama began. At first, it seemed to be good. Then he started to control and isolate me from everyone. I couldn't go anywhere and if I did and took too long he would physically abuse me. I wasn't allowed to go to school, work or anything. I remember going to the store and I took too long so he thought. When I arrived at the house, He questioned why I took so long. Then he spit in my face.

He would act one way in the church and different at home. It was so disgusting he would have me pray in the church with him, and then have sex with me in the church. He introduced me to sexual acts that were unbelievable and made me sick to my stomach. He would have me in the house and have sex with other young girls from the church while I was living there. I was afraid of him and it felt like I was under some demonic spell and I could not get away from him.

He would abuse me at home. When I went to church, I better have on my church face ready to play the part of the first lady. I knew my place. I knew what to do and what not to do. This abuse continued for some time. So, our church would fellowship with another church, and there were a group of women at this church. Of all the women, I connected with one woman. I was extremely afraid of telling her my dilemma. How do you tell someone that you're being abused by the pastor? He had me living with him pretending to be married to me.

For some reason this woman seemed to know what I was going through, and I would talk with her every time we went to this church. Eventually I told her everything and this was the beginning of me fighting for my freedom. I reached out for help and used my voice. I left him, but it wasn't easy. I was bound with demonic forces. My mother and aunt prayed for me daily until the strongholds were completely broken.

It was a continual cycle of me leaving and going back. When I left, I felt as if he was working witchcraft on me. I could not sleep in my own bed; I was tormented and would have nightmares. Once you break away from hurt and abuse, if you don't get healed it perpetuates. After this ordeal, I continued to enter relationships that were not productive for my life. I was broken and needed to be healed. You may wonder why people stay in relationships that are abusive. It's an evil spirit that holds you in captivity, and with the intent to keep you in prison, never letting you go free.

Life Lessons

I learned that you cannot trust everyone who says, "Lord." Before you join a church, make sure you pray and ask God to show you the character of the pastor. Anytime you confide in a man of God and he starts crossing boundaries run away from that ministry. Finally, be careful how much you share in your counseling sessions. predators use your weakness to exploit and manipulate.

Accomplishments

You must fight for your life and for the life of your children. I started to reach out for support and surrounded myself with praying people. I will say when God sets you free you are free indeed. I'm currently married to a wonderful praying man who loves me dearly and we have a beautiful daughter. My first daughter is grown, and I have three beautiful grandchildren. I have gained my own independence and have a wonderful career. If you are in the church, and in an abusive relationship please reach out for support and help.

Chapter Seven

The Silent Epidemic

One of the many secrets that exist in the church is domestic violence. Women are increasingly becoming victims at the hand of leaders in spiritual authority. Many of these women are afraid to speak out because their husbands are in powerful positions and they feel like they will not be heard or taken seriously. Because there is a stigma associated with domestic violence many are silent. It is my desire for you to speak out. Domestic Violence is physical, emotional (psychological) and spiritually draining. My name is Allie, and this is my story. I am a victor which makes me *victorious.*

As I look back over my life I would have never imagined that I would have gone through so much in my life to be so victorious today. My younger years were not the best, but I know my mom did the best that she could. I will be forever grateful.

At the age of 14, I lost my virginity; at the age of 16 I had my first child. Then at the age of 21, I had my second child, and not long after I was pregnant again and decided to have an abortion. I had another one about a year after that. At the age of 31, I decided to have a Tuba Ligation, because having two children was enough for me especially because I was a single parent. My mom raised my oldest daughter since I was so young and still in high school and I wasn't being the mother to my daughter that I should have been.

I never had that male role model or father figure. I was the youngest of four in my family and none of my siblings ever sat me down to discuss anything about growing up (the do's and don'ts). At the age of 19, I was in my first abusive relationship with my oldest daughter's father. He thought that he could just do whatever he wanted to do to me He cheated on me, raped me twice, and once was at knife point. He broke into my house both times and hid in my closet. No means NO regardless of who they are. When I did approach him and asked if he was cheating on me, he proceeded to assault me by trying to choke me, and kicked me in my stomach and chest, fracturing 3 of my ribs and putting me into convulsions. The only thing that allowed him to be prosecuted was the fact that a neighbor saw the whole thing and testified in this case.

Throughout my life I felt like I was always trying to find that father figure in a relationship. When the only father that I needed was My Heavenly Father. So, at the age of 42, I accepted the Lord as my Savior, joined FCFM in Burlington, New Jersey where I have been since March 7, 2010 and serve as a Deaconess in my ministry.

I have been in a few different relationships on and off, however, nothing serious until I met this man in February of 2012. I was minding my own business, doing my laundry with my daughter and granddaughter; when suddenly, this dark chocolate man appears just looking at me smiling like he could just devour me. I was then approached by him and he asked if anyone was sitting in the chair next to me, I responded, “No, you can sit here.”

He had a smile that would light up the room and Lord knows my flesh was weak and I was feeling way. Well, we exchanged numbers. After we had a nice discussion and found out that we were both serving in our own ministries at church, I thought this man was Heaven sent. Little did I know, I was in for the ride of my life and he was a wolf in sheep's clothing. We started going to dinner, the movies, doing family things together, and then we also started worshipping together at each other's churches.

A few of my church family told me it didn't look good. But I always said, "I don't know what you're talking about," But they knew otherwise.

We continued to see each other, spent a lot of time together, and even moved in together. I knew it was a wrong. He had been separated from his wife for some time but was still legally married. I didn't let that bother me because I just knew he was going to get divorced. "He isn't even mine to have, but no I just continued seeing him, even though GOD was not pleased.

I saw all the signs that weren't good from this man. He was very controlling, needed to know my every move. I couldn't even stop at the store on the way home from work without him calling to see where I was. This man threatened to bring another woman into our home; and was always throwing my past in my face. This man was supposed to be a minister, yet my past was really bothering him. I just couldn't understand that. You would have thought that it was still my present issues.

I really tried to work things out with this man. I had to have double foot surgery on September 5, 2013, we were already living together, and I had to rely on him to take me back and forth to work for 4-6 weeks (total control now). One morning we went to breakfast at IHOP and got into a heated discussion. I can't even remember what it was about, but what I do know is that this man raised his voice at me several times and I just got angry. When we were on our way home from breakfast, I decided to get out of the car at the next traffic light and walk home, yes walk home.

It took hours for me to walk home. A few people wanted to take me home, but I said, "No thank you, I need to pray this situation away, but thank you."

My dear Sister in Christ, Minister Stephanie stayed with me on the phone almost the whole way home. I love my sister and thank God for her. By the time I got home, my feet were so swollen and hurting so bad, keep in mind it had only been three weeks since my surgery.

On New Year's Day January 1, 2014, I made him breakfast so when he came in from work he could eat something hot and lay down to get some rest. Well, I really can't tell you exactly what happened but the man "snapped once again. He said that I was trying to poison him and threw out his breakfast and everything that was in the freezer and refrigerator.

I tell you there was something seriously wrong with this man; he seemed like Dr. Jekyll and Mr. Hyde. I really didn't know at times who I was talking to. Yet I continued and stayed. I really tried, I realized that I had to help myself because I truly was dying inside. My self-esteem went out the window and I didn't recognize myself anymore. My pastor was constantly praying for me, but God kept me during it all. BUT GOD!

Things went on for awhile in our situation because it was just that a situation. Being in this situation I really thought that this man would change for the better, but he hid his Hennessy bottles all over house. I would pour them out when I found them, and he got very angry. He also kept a machete by the bed. He would curse at me as well. I tried counseling within his church, but it seemed like it got flipped on me like I was the problem. We had one session and this man never even admitted that he had an anger problem. We both agreed that we needed to separate. Although we still tried to work it out. God said, "Keep your distance." The relationship was finally over, the agony, torment, and pain. I found the courage to embrace my freedom and take my life back.

Embracing My Freedom

First, I had to admit I had a problem. If you can't admit it, then you are in denial. I thank God for my past. It has made me a stronger woman today. I'm not happy about it, but my past is just that, "My Past."

I have come out on top and I have bounced back better than ever. My light shines bright and my heart sings, "Hallelujah." When I finally came to my senses and went back to my home church family, they were so happy to see me, but inside I was still struggling with a lot of mess. Although I was free from the relationship, it was a very traumatic experience. I continued to deal with internal struggles such as hurt, pain, trust, feelings of loneliness, abandonment, low self-esteem, anger, and not feeling worthy of anything. I just wasn't sure of me anymore. I put so much into the relationship trying to make it work, but I probably did more than I should have, and I stayed too long.

I was too mentally, physically and emotionally drained and barely holding on. When you're coming out of a traumatic experience, you must surround yourself with people who love and care about you. As I continued to be around the people who loved me, I gained so much strength. I did not seclude or isolate myself. I reached out to those I knew would be encouraging to me. Deep down inside my heart I kept telling myself to let it go, but time just kept passing me by and eventually the pain went away. I forgave myself and I also forgave him. I'm determined that I WILL NOT SETTLE FOR LESS. God has a perfect plan for me and I deserve the best. To date, I have continued to move forward, serving the Lord; He is the strength of my life, and my everything.

Life Lesson

As I look back over my past I have asked myself what got me into these situations anyway? I really have no idea, but what I can tell you is that I know the signs today of what I WILL NOT accept in any relationship:

- Embarrassing me and calling me names out of my character
- Intimidating me
- Controlling what I do, who I talk to, where I go, how to dress, wear my hair or color my nails
- Act like the abuse is no big deal or it is my fault, or even deny doing it

We all deserve to be treated with respect, feel valued and be safe. Emotionally abusive relationships can destroy your self-worth, lead to anxiety and depression and make you feel helpless and alone. No one should have to endure this kind of pain – your first step to breaking free is recognizing that your situation is abusive. Once you acknowledge the reality of the abusive situation, then you can get the help that you need.

An Attitude of Gratitude

I just want to first give Glory and Honor to God for saving me during it all and allowing me to be part of such a special project. I could never have imagined God using me like this. Thank you, Sheri Durricks for your vision and allowing me to be part of that vision.

Encouragement

To all of those who have been hurt or are currently in a situation and you feel as though there is no way out, trust in God Almighty. Reach out for help and pray to God for Wisdom and Guidance. I told you that I was so unsure about myself once I left this relationship. Abuse will make you doubt that there is any good left in you, so you must reprogram your mind. Here is an exercise to help you. Fill in the blanks:

Name 5 of your greatest qualities?

____

____

____

____

____

What are 4 things you know that you are good at doing?

____

____

____

____

____

I always dreamed of doing or becoming what?

____

____

____

____

____

Before I got in this relationship I use to do what?

Now that I'm free, I will begin to...

I will seek healing from: therapy, self-help books, church, etc.

Chapter Eight

Starting Over

Don't start your Day with the broken pieces of yesterday. Every morning you wake up is the first day of the rest of your life-Author Unknown

If you are reading this book, it is apparent that you're seeking for something other than what you're experiencing now. Know this, today is your day for a new beginning. Are you in abusive relationship and afraid to leave? Perhaps you have been in this thing so long and you don't know where to start. You have children and your significant other is your sole provider. You relocated from another state and don't know where to go. I am quite sure there are many circumstances that may hinder you from moving forward. There are countless other women just like you. You read about them in this book and we are living proof that you can begin again this is what FACES is all about Finally taking Action, conquering your Fears, embracing your Freedom and Standing in Your Authority.

Take Action

It is necessary that you have a plan of exit that is not easily noticed by your abuser. The National Domestic Violence Hotline suggests following these steps to improve your chances of leaving safely:

- **Know the number to your local women's shelter.** This can be obtained through a simple Google search at your local library. If you use your own computer, make sure that you clear the cookies so that your search history won't be traced
- **Reach out for support**. This step

is vitally important. You cannot do this alone and will need help from those who you can really trust. Use code words that are not easily detected and understood or visual signals such as the house light, on means no danger, off means, I need assistance. Determine the codes that are easy to remember.

- **Document all violent** incidents such as bruises cuts etc., take pictures and keep in discreet locations. You may want to secure a postal box at your local post office.

- **Devise a plan:** Make sure to include your children and insure them it is your duty to make sure they are safe. Identify where your will stay and how you will leave.

Recently, I had a friend who was in a marriage for 31 years and she wanted to get out of the relationship. She wanted to leave for some time, so she carefully planned everything. She kept up her normal routine so that nothing seemed out of the ordinary. During the time he was at work, she sought for a lawyer and received all the legal advice she needed. If the lawyer needed to mail anything, it was sent to another address. She knew his work schedule and routine. While he was working each night, she would take clothes out of her closet and take them to a friend's house. She did it so that it would not be noticeable.

When you are starting over, you don't need to take everything with you. Remember you're starting over. You can always get things back, but it's important to leave safely. Long story short, when she left he was at work. When he finally discovered what was happening, he was already served with divorce papers from the lawyer. He had no idea she was going to leave. Why? She carefully planned everything.

At first, she would text me. I told her to stop texting me and to converse with me through email because he did not have her email or password. She started her life completely over. In fact, she had been with this guy since she was 18 years old and is now 55, so you can imagine the fear she had to conquer. The fear of paying bills on her own because he took care of everything, obtaining her own place and just stepping into a new world of going from married to single. She moved to another location many miles from where she lived and is doing very well.

- ❖ If you have a car, always keep it fuel in case you must make an abrupt escape. Always keep an extra key in a safe place that will be easy to obtain.

- Have an emergency bag packed and keep at a friend, family member, or job. Make sure that you have all important items, toiletries, and medications if needed. Keep water and plenty of snacks in your trunk.

Keep in mind to use cash for everything so that your purchases and credit card will not be traced. For more safety tips Contact the National Domestic Hotline 1-800-799-safe. Your call is safe and all information that you give will be held in strict confidence. The hotline will assist you with safe housing in your area. These houses are called safe houses because when you reside in one you 're forbidden to tell anyone where you live. I was not only a victim of domestic violence, but I have assisted many women with safety plans to leave their abuser and helped them get into safe housing. You can do this. God will lead you safely out and lead you in the right direction. Have faith and believe.

Conquering My Fears

Think of a situation that makes you utterly afraid of failure, and then visualize yourself encountering barriers, hindrances and obstacles. Allow yourself to experience all the emotions that you will feel. Suddenly see yourself moving passed those obstacles. Next, think about how you intend to overcome those obstacles and write it down.

What are my major obstacles?

____

____

____

____

____

What is my plan to move past these obstacles?

____

____

____

____

____

Conquering your fears can be intimidating all by itself. Fear causes you to have racing thoughts, so to conqueror these thoughts you must take time out for yourself. Start by taking a hot bath, listening to nice soothing music, reading a book, or talking to a friend. Once your mind is clear you will notice that some of your fears have decreased and you can easily move forward. This is not an easy task, so you must keep practicing and it will become easier.

Embrace My Freedom

Every individual has their own concept of freedom. What freedom means to me may mean something totally different to you. Freedom is not something you just think about, but it is an idea.

What does freedom mean to you?

____
____
____
____

Imagine where you are right now in your current relationship. Describe what freedom looks like. Include feelings, taste, smell, colors, object, etc.

____
____

____

____

Remember freedom does not come easy and you must do the work. Many believe that Jesus died on the Cross for the sins of man. He paid the ultimate price for our freedom. Harriet Tubman paid a price helping slaves to become free. Martin Luther King lost his life fighting and advocating for freedom. What are you willing to do, so that you can embrace your freedom?

____

____

____

____

Stand in Your Authority

You have the right to exercise your authority. Before you were created God already had you in mind. He gave you gifts, talents and abilities to be everything He created you to be. Jesus spoke on one occasion to His disciples and said, "I have given you power over scorpions and serpents and over ALL the POWER OF the ENEMY and NOTHING shall by ANY MEANS HARM OR HURT YOU."

This simply means that you have power over any negative thoughts, behavior or evil forces that you encounter, or that that is inside of you. If it's fear, doubt, or unbelief, you have the right to command and determine your direction. When you boldly speak and affirm positive things in your life, you are letting the universe know that you will not accept anything less than God's best in your life.

God wants you to decree a thing and it will be established. When you accept Christ into your life as your personal savior, you enter an eternal and unbreakable covenant with God. Currently, all His promises are available to you if you receive them by faith.

When declarations of his Word are spoken over your life, the Word is then activated to strengthen your spirit man and prepare you for an intimate relationship with Him and for every good blessing that he has for you. His Word will never ever come back to him empty. It is sure to accomplish everything that it is sent to do. What is it that you need done right now this very moment? I dare you to believe God and watch what He will do.

You may be reading this book and have a broken fellowship with God. Or you may be reading this and say I want you to experience walking in these blessings, promises and authority that God has for me. Where do I start? Perhaps you believe in nothing at all and feel like you don't need religion. Well, that's good news!!! I am simply offering you a life changing experience by experiencing a personal one on one relationship with your heavenly father. Let's start today. Simply pray this prayer:

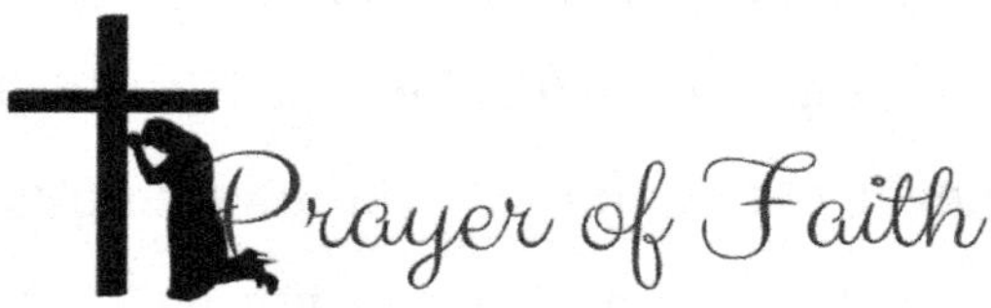

Dear God,

I know that I'm not perfect. I know I am not where you want me to be, and I want your forgiveness. I believe that you have a purpose for my life and that it was completed when your Son paid the price for my wrong doings.

Please wash me clean from all guilt, sin, and shame and come into my heart. I believe by faith thank you for all you are going to do. My life will never be the same.

Conclusion

Domestic violence is a serious issue and it is also deemed a crime. If you are currently in a relationship that is abusive and fear for your life reach out for help. Ladies, our journey ends here. This is the conclusion of this book, but a brand-new beginning for you. You have read the stories of the survivors who have been where you are. Each one of you reading this book has one woman in this book that you can relate to. Our stories are your stories. It is with great hope and faith that you will now take the next step and use your voice.

Every time you feel hopeless read how each woman overcame their abuse. Remember this will not be easy and you will face difficult challenges every day but know that you are not alone. I commend you for taking the first step. You are brave and courageous. The decision you make today will determine your entire future. You already have everything you need on the inside to take you to places you could never imagine. Remember FACES encourages you to finally take Action to Conqueror your Fears, embrace your Freedom and Stand in your God-given Authority.

References

www.newchoicesinc.org/help/DV/signs

www.domesticviolence.com.au/pages/impact-of-domestic-violence-on-women.php

www.sinbysilence.com/pressmaterials/dvfacts.html

www.uschess.org/content/view/9111/28/

www.naimawilliams.com/blog/2009/06/23/spirit-of-intimidation-a-big-problem-least-acknowledged/

www.newagefraud.org/smf/index.php?topic=2225.0

ww.overcomingpowerlessness.com/affirmations.htm

www.thehopeofsurvivors.com/news_notes/not_an_affair.php

http://awomanscornd.blogspot.com/2009/06/art-of-seduction-seducers.html

www.bhevolution.org/public/overcoming_shame_based_thinking.page

www.businessdictionary.com/definition/abuse-of-power.html

ww.snapnetwork.org/psych_effects/soul_stealing_1.ht

http://womenslaw.org/

www.melanietoniaevans.com/services/narc-abuse-recovery.htm

Credits

Contributing Stories:

Author: Sheri Durricks, MHS, LCADC

Christina D.

Lyric Ashley

Talaya Holiday

Allie Cordero

Business Coach/Book Consultant:

Shalena D.I.V.A.

Book Cover Design-

BevCottondesign.com

Photography: Ed Ward, III- Legacy Studio

Makeup Artist: Lydia Ward

Hair Stylist: Evette Jefferson

About the Author

Sheri Durricks grew up in Philadelphia She witnessed much gang, drugs activity, and violence in her neighborhood. She currently resides in New Jersey, and work as a Licensed Therapist for those addicted to drugs and alcohol. During her career, Sheri has mentored, coached, and empowered, young adolescent females and women of all cultures for over twenty years. These women have experienced many types of trauma in the form of sexual assault, domestic violence, psychological abuse, self-abuse, and traumatic events. Because of working with this population, a women's group was formed to assist women who experienced all types of trauma with tools, resources and life skills.

Sheri was also a recovery mentor for women who are addicted to heroin and other substances. Sheri received her master's Degree at Lincoln University for Human Services and Counseling and she is currently enrolled at Walden University pursing her PhD for Human Services specializing in Social Policy Analysis and Planning. She was recently inducted into the Tau Upsilon Alpha- Alpha Chi Chapter in recognition of academic and professional excellence in Human Services. In addition, she is a certified domestic violence and sexual assault specialist. Sheri is also the founder and CEO of House of Refuge for Women registered in New Jersey, She is in the process of establishing it as a transitional house for women. Sheri has spoken at numerous churches and women conferences. Sheri is a Change Agent, and her mission is to help empower women to break the shackles of low self-esteem, to safety and freedom by discovering their purpose in life. The Many Faces of Domestic Violence was recently created as extensions of the Beauty 4 ur Ashes to reach women who are in abusive, dysfunctional relationships. The Faces represent women from all cultural spectrums that don't visibly show signs of abuse such as black eye, or broken bones, but they have invisible scars and they are your corporate leaders, first ladies and parishioners in the church, doctors, or even the girl next door.

I'm here to assist you with reconnecting first with the real authentic you, and the reason why you were place on the earth (Purpose) Yes, I know it's been tough and you've been through much. However, YOU are NOT what you been through, so let do this, exchange Beauty 4 your Ashes. Think about the caterpillar that goes through difficult stages just to transition into that beautiful butterfly. Butterflies are a symbol of transitions because of their phenomenal ability to change from one stage to the next. You are at your next stage of transition...

For workshops, speaking engagement or conferences you can connect me at the following:

https://www.facebook.com/Sheri-Durricks-635446773231814

https://about.me/Destine2bGreat

Website:

www.sheridbeauty4urashes.com

Email:

meetme@sheridbeauty4urashes.com

Made in the USA
Columbia, SC
06 December 2023

27903382R00104